VALIANT IMPERIAL WARRIORS
2200 YEARS AGO
—Terra-cotta Armoured Warriors and Horses of
Qin Shi Huang Mausoleum

2000. 12. 2.

PREFACE

In the early spring of 1974, a number of peasants from Xiyang Village of Yanzhai Township in Lintong County accidentally discovered some ancient bronze weapons and pieces of broken terra-cotta armoured warriors while sinking a well at the northern foot of Mt. Lishan 35 km. of Xi'an, the famous cultural city in China's history. No one had ever expected that this accidental discovery would turn over a most miraculous and brilliant leaf in China's archaeology, add another wonderous sight to the history of human civilization and unfold a unique and majestic spectacle before world.

After years of drilling, excavation and textual research, the site was proved to be an attendant burial pit of the huge army of the terra-cotta armoured warriors and horses in the mausoleum of China's first feudal emperor Qin Shi Huang. By 1976 three such pits had been found. They were numbered Pits 1, 2 and 3 respectively in order of discovery, with a total area of over 20,000 sq.m. where were buried nearly 8,000 terra-cotta armoured warriors and horses, and more than 100 chariots. The pits, containing a rectangular battle formation of infantry and chariots in the first, an L-shaped composite formation of infantry, cavalry and charioteers in the second and a command post of the huge underground army in the third, are closely related as an integral whole, though separated from and independent to one another. They reproduce an imposing and grandiose scene of the Qin army one million strong with 1,000 chariots and 10,000 horses in the battlefields.

Before long the excavation of the three pits became known far and wide, stirred up a sensation across the world and enjoyed a prestige of being "an archaeological discovery of top importance of this century", "the Eighth Wonder of the World" and one of China's best scenic spots. In 1987 the UNESCO placed Qin Shi Huang Mausoleum and the terra-cotta armoured warriors and horses among the world's cultural legacies. This fully manifests that they are not only the cultural legacies of the Chinese nation, but also the rare treasures of the mankind at large. They take up a splendid place in the history of human civilization.

1. *Sketch Map on Qin Shi Huang Mausoleum and Pits of Terra-cotta Armoured Warriors and Horses*

2. *Sketch Map on Locations of Numbered Pits 1, 2 and 3*

3. *Bird's-eye View of Museum of Terra-cotta Armoured Warriors and Horses*

4. *Exterior of Museum of Terra-cotta Armoured Warriors and Horses*

5. *Full View of No.1 Pit*

3

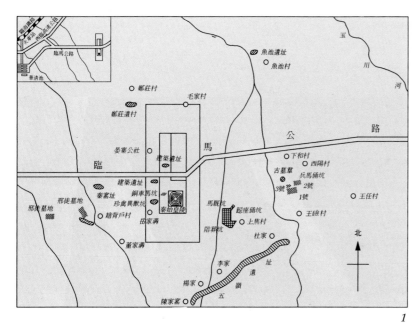

1

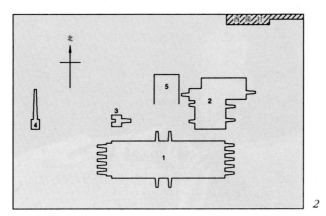

2

4

5

3

QIN SHI HUANG AND HIS MAUSOLEUM

Qin Shi Huang (259-210 B.C.) was the first emperor of the Qin Dynasty (221-206 B.C.). He was an all-powerful and meritorious feudal emperor of great talent and bold vision in China's history. He was also the founder of China's first big and multi-national centralized feudal empire. He came to the world at the late stage in the Warring States Period (475-221 B.C.), when battles were fought among separationist vassals, particularly those among seven feudal states for overlordship. The family name of his was Ying and the given name, Zheng. He mounted the throne at the age of 13 and took the helm of the state in person when he reached 22. In his endeavour to strengthen the national might by a big margin, he carried out political reforms, adopted policies of promoting farm work and expanding military strength, appointed people of talent to proper posts and put the army under rigorous training. All that helped him to sweep away one after another his six rival states of Han (424-230 B.C.), Zhao (475-222 B.C.), Yan (11th century-222 B.C.), Wei (445-225 B.C.), Chu (11th century-223 B.C.) and Qi (11th century-221 B.C.) in the ten-year-long battles from 230 to 221 B.C. Thus, he put an end to the chaos of several hundred years after the Spring and Autumn Period (770-476 B.C.) and established the Qin Dynasty — the first unified feudal state in China's history. In order to consolidate the new-born feudal regime, he thoroughly abolished the fief system that existed in the Dynasties of Shang (16th - 11th century B.C.) and Zhou (11th century-221 B.C.) and thereafter by implementation of the administrative system at the level of prefecture and county. Apart from that, he placed three ministers and nine high court officials in the central government. So, an entirely new regime was taken shape with his grip on important military and political powers. He ordered the legal codes, currencies, written languages, axle lengths of carts, and weights and measures to be unified throughout the state. At his order the Great Wall began to be built, and the imperial thoroughfares, paved. He commanded his army to subdue the southern tribes and repulse the invasion by the Huns from the north. Moreover, he initiated the title of Emperor as the top ruler of the state and proclaimed himself the First Emperor. Bold and resolute, these unprecedented reform measures and iron-handed doings played a big role in the development of the feudal economy and exerted far-reaching influences on the generations to follow. Nevertheless, Qin Shi Huang was a brutal autocrat. To tighten his totalitarian rule and live a luxurious life of extravagance and dissipation, he inflicted cruel tortures and inexorable penalties, extorted excessive taxes and levies, and conducted military operations for years running. He devastated culture by burning books and burying Confucian scholars alive. Consequently, the economy was driven into stagnancy and the people eked out a meagre existence. In face of the widespread popular resentment, he was bogged down in crisis. The Qin Dynasty under his rule, a feudal state once so lively and unchallengeable, became the shortest-lived feudal dynasty that lasted only 15 years.

Qin Shi Huang cherished superstitious beliefs in longevity. More than once he dispatched alchemists, with several thousand children in their early teens under their command, to search for a longevous medicine in the East China Sea. On the other hand, he began the construction of a mausoleum for himself at the foot of Mt. Lishan when he ascended the throne at the age of 13. As was recorded in China's historical books, the mausoleum was a project of immense size. Labourers and convicts conscribed in the construction totalled as many as 720,000 in a period of 37 years. The project was not entirely completed when the emperor died. As was depicted in the *Book of the Han Dynasty*, Qin Shi Huang Mausoleum *"was built deep into the ground, and the mound above was close to 170 metres high with a circumference of 2.5 km. Inside the tomb the sarcophagus was afloat on a mercury sea, lit by lamps burning human fat and dotted with gold wild geese. It was unparalleled in number of rare treasures, variation of mechanical devices, magnificence of the coffin and grandeur of the halls and chambers."* From the above, it is obvious that the interior of the mausoleum was in all senses a grand and gorgeous underground palace. The preliminary data obtained through archaeological excavation and drilling reveal that Qin Shi Huang Mausoleum covers an area of 56.25 sq.km., surrounded by two enclosures in rectangular shape. The inner city measures 580 m. in latitude and 1,355 m. in longtitude, with a circumference of 3,870 m. The outer city measures 940 m. widthwise and 2,165 m. lengthwise, with a circumference of 6,210 m. Both the inner and outer cities have a gate and a watchtower on each of the four sides, with corner towers at the four angles of the inner city. The mound lying in the southern half of the inner city was about 115 m. high originally. In spite of exposure to weather over 2,000 years, it is still more than 70 m. above the ground. Below it is the underground palace where Qin Shi Huang rested in his coffin. It remains unknown how many jewels and curios were hidden in the palace. But a large number of precious historical relics were unearthed in the several hundred attendant burial pits that had been discovered around the mausoleum. These include the pits containing the symbolic bronze chariots and horses used by the emperor, the rare birds and animals from the enclosures where the emperor went hunting and sought for amusement, the palatial stables as well as pottery figures in kneeling and sitting postures, burial tombs for immolated slaves and builders of the mausoleum. Among them all, the pits of the terra-cotta armoured warriors and horses stand out in dazzling brilliance. From what was made known, the underground palace of Qin Shi Huang Mausoleum is a true reproduction of the kingdom above the ground that has ever existed in human history, and the terra-cotta armoured warriors and horses are symbols of the crack army defending the capital of the Qin Dynasty.

◁7、Map on Domain of Qin Dynasty

8B、A Bronze Tripod runearthed in Qin Shi Huang Mausoleum
(59.6cm in Hight 212kg in weight.)

▽8A、The stone Armouts unearthed in
Qin shi Huang Mausoleum

8C、A Stone Helmet unearthed in Qin Shi Huang Mausoleum

8D、The bare-armed Terra-cotta Warriors unearthed in Qin Shi Huang Mausoleum

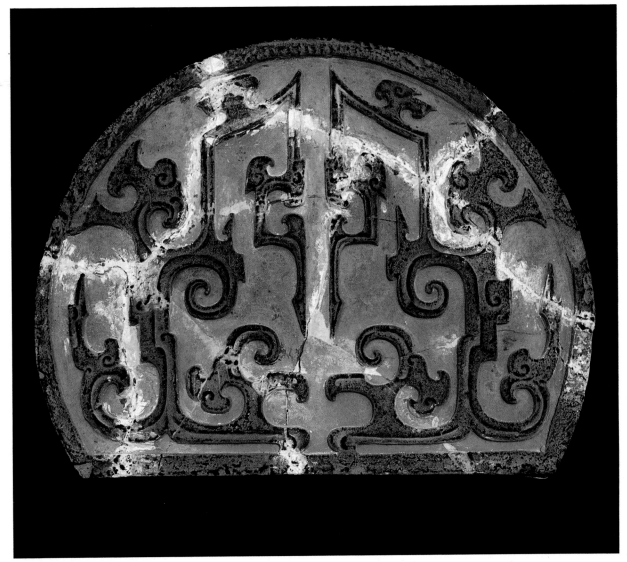

9

IMMENSE AND MAGNIFICENT UNDERGROUND MILITARY MUSEUM

The burial pits of the terra-cotta armoured warriors and horses are situated about 1.5 km. to the east of the mausoleum mound. This location was not mentioned in any of China's historical books. Rich in ancient military concepts, they are well rated as an underground military museum of great immensity and magnificence.

The No.1 Pit consists of a rectangular battle formation of charioteers and infantrymen. Measured 14,260 sq.m. in total with 230 m. widthwise and 62 m. lengthwise, the pit is estimated to contain over 6,000 terra-cotta armoured warriors and horses, including the vanguard, the main body, the flanks and the rear guard. At the eastern end of the pit lies a gallery where stand facing east three rows of terra-cotta archers in battle tunics and puttees, 68 in each row. Holding crossbows and arrows in hands, they have their hair tied back and no helmets on. As valiant and excellent archers, they constitute the vanguard. Behind the gallery, rammed partition walls divided the No.1 Pit into 11 latitudinal passage-ways where stand facing east 38 columns of warriors with horse-drawn chariots deployed in a regular pattern. Most of the warriors are armour-clad, holding such weapons as spears, barbed spears, long spears, halberds or crossbows. As heavily-armed warriors, they make up the main body in the No.1 Pit and represent the principal force of the Qin army. Apart from that, along the pit's edges to the south, north and west stands a row of armoured warriors facing south, north and west correspondingly. They are the flanks and the rear guard, ready to beat back flank attacks from possible enemies. The battle formation is well-organized. The partial excavation conducted so far in the No.1 Pit has uncovered 1,000 odd terra-cotta armoured warriors, 8 chariots and 32 terra-cotta horses. So, more details of this battle formation will be known only when the excavation is completed.

The No.2 Pit is located 20 m. to the north of the eastern end of the No.1 Pit. The formal excavation has not yet begun. As is known through drilling and test excavation at a few points, the pit is L-shaped, 124 m. long and 98 m. wide, with a coverage of nearly 6,000 sq.m. It contains over 1,300 terra-cotta armoured warriors and horses together with about 90 wooden chariots in a battle formation of a mixed army of infantry, cavalry and chariots. The formation is made up of four small arrays. The first, situated in the front of the L-shaped battle formation, is the array of 174 standing archers in battle tunics and 160 kneeling archers in armour, all holding crossbows. The standing archers are placed on the outer flanks whereas the kneeling ones are in the center. In real combats, the two kinds of archers alternate their postures and shoot by turns with arrows showering upon attackers. To the right of the L-shape is the second array composed of 64 chariots, each of which carries three warriors. The third array consisting of chariots, infantry and cavalry is a column formation in the middle of the L-shaped army. This array, with 19 chariots as the main force aided by a small number of infantrymen and cavalrymen, is on mobile manoeuvre. To the left of the L-shaped formation is the fourth and last array made up mainly of 100 odd cavalrymen on saddled horses in a rectangular pattern.

The battle formation in the No.2 Pit is by far more complicated than that in the No.1 Pit. It consists of smaller arrays and camps enclosed by bigger ones, which are interrelated and in symmetrical shape. The mixed formation of charioteers, infantry and cavalry was in particular an important development and change in the army disposition as compared with that of the Warring States Period when the latter two were independent armed services.

The No.3 Pit is located 25 m. to the north of the western end of the No.1 Pit and 120 m. to the east of the No.2 Pit. The plane of the pit is of concave shape totalling about 500 sq.m., with a measurement of 17.6 m. from east to west and 21.4 m. from north to south. Out of the pit was unearthed one wooden chariot, four terra-cotta horses and 68 terra-cotta armoured warriors. The warriors are not arranged in a battle formation, but stand opposite to each other in two rows after the pattern of the guard of honour. They hold bamboo weapons with pointed heads for self-defence. Unearthed also in this pit were deer-horns and animal bones left behind after sacrificial offerings and war prayers. This clearly shows that the No.3 Pit contains most likely not an ordinary battle formation but the command post directing the mighty underground army.

Ancient weapons were also discovered in large quantities during the excavation in the pits of the terra-cotta armoured warriors. Among the Qin weapons unearthed are short weapons such as swords and scimitars, long-shafted weapons such as spears, barbed spears, halberds, bamboo weapons with pointed heads and long spears, and long-range weapons such as cross-bow triggers and arrow-heads, totalling tens of thousands in a dozen varieties. They were mostly made of bronze, except for a few iron ones. Almost all the varieties of the weapons once used by the Qin warriors can be seen in these pits. These bronze weapons, though buried underground for over 2,000 years, still glitter in metallic lustre when the mud was removed. The one-metre-long sword is especially impressive for sharp edge and back gauge. A mere glance at it will remind visitors of a few lines from a poem written by Li Bai, the well-known poet of the Tang Dynasty:

The Qin emperor swept his six rivals in the way,
With imposing air that commanded awe and respect.
A thrust by the sword drove the messy clouds away,
And the vassals all paid homage to the west.

Scientific and technical examination reveals that the unearthed weapons contain such metallic elements as copper, lead, tin, zinc and nickel. The swords and the arrow-heads are coated with a thin layer of oxidated chromium, which proves that the weapons were oxidated with chromate in the making. But it was not until modern times that this anti-erosion and anti-rust technology was mastered by European countries and the United States. This can not but be a miracle in the history of metallurgical industry and a convincing proof of the advanced technology in ancient China.

The pits of the terra-cotta armoured warriors and horses make up a tremendous underground military camp, in which are placed valiant soldiers and generals, metal weapons and stalwart horses, as well as military staff that make strategies. The discovery provides rich ancient military information and data by the most reliable and vivid objects passed down through the history to facilitate the study of military concepts, battle formations, army dispositions, military equipment and sources of warriors in the Qin Dynasty. It is by no means an exaggeration to say that standing before the pits of the terra-cotta armoured warriors and horses one would feel as if he was reviewing the Qin army of over 2,000 years ago.

10. Vanguard of Battle
Formation in No.1 Pit

10

14

13. *Back View of Battle Array*
    in No.1 Pit
14. *Front View of Battle Array*
    in No.1 Pit

15

16

19

20

21

23

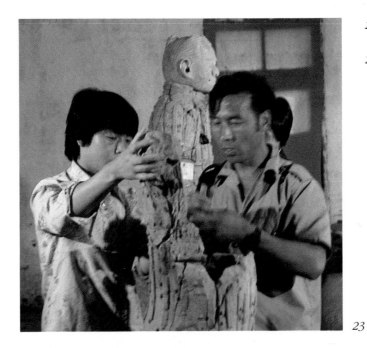

22. *Excavation of Terra-cotta Figures*

23. 24. *Terra-cotta Figures under Repair*

23

24

25

25. *Terra-cotta Officers and Warriors*

26. *A Repaired Terra-cotta Warriors Being Hoisted to Original Place*

25

26

27

28

28

29

30. *A Terra-cotta Charioteer*

31. *Subordinate Terra-cotta Infantrymen before and behind a Chariot*

32. *Back View of Terra-cotta Vanguard Warriors in No.1 Pit*

31

32

33. *Back View of Part of No.1 Pit*

34. *Head of a Terra-cotta Horse*

35. *A Terra-cotta Horse*

34

35

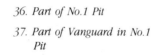

36. Part of No.1 Pit

37. Part of Vanguard in No.1 Pit

36

38. *Subordinate Terra-cotta Infantrymen before and behind a Chariot*

39. *Terra-cotta Warriors in Armour and in Battle Tunics*

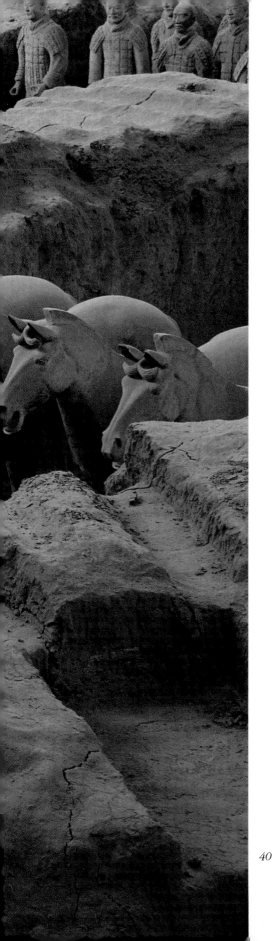

40-41. *Subordinate Terra-cotta
Infantrymen before and
behind a Chariot*

42. *Terra-cotta Horses and
Remains of a Chariot*

41

42

40

43. Remains of a Chariot and
    Battle Array

44. A Terra-cotta Charioteer

43

45. *Terra-cotta Figure and*
    Terra-cotta Horses

46. *Back View of Chariot*
    Remains

47. *Array of Terra-cotta
    Warriors*

48. *Back View of Terra-cotta
    Horses and Terra-cotta
    Figures*

47

48

49. *Front View of Terra-cotta Armoured Warriors*

50. *Back View of Terra-cotta Armoured Warriors*

51. *Right Flank of Battle Formation in No.1 Pit*

52. *Left Flank of Battle Formation in No.1 Pit*

49

50

51

52

53. Exterior of NO.2 Pit

54A. Raffer Remains in the Pit of
   Terra−Cotta Figures

54 B
54 C   *Excavation of No.2 Pit*

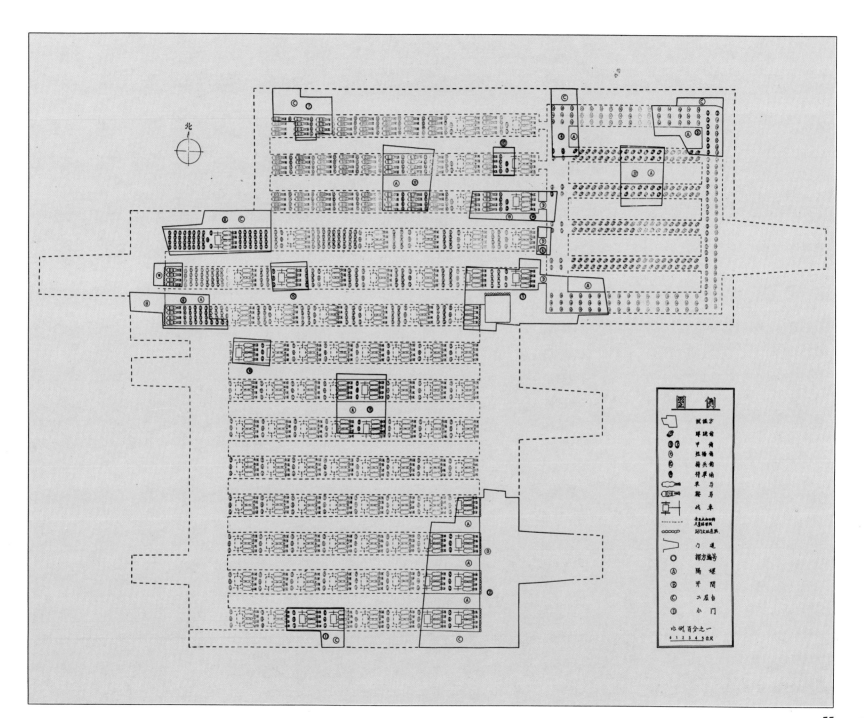

北

图例

試掘方
陶俑角
平頂角
弩兵衛俑
特軍与
束弩号
戎車

門道
探方編号
陽燧
開間
二層台
小門

比例百分之一
0 1 2 3 4 5公尺

55. *Lay-out in No.2 Pit and Unearthed Sketch Map on Military Dispositions*

56. *A Terra-cotta Kneeling Archer Excavated in No.2 Pit*

56

57. *Full View of No.3 Pit*
58. *Excavation of Northern*
    Chamber in No.3 Pit

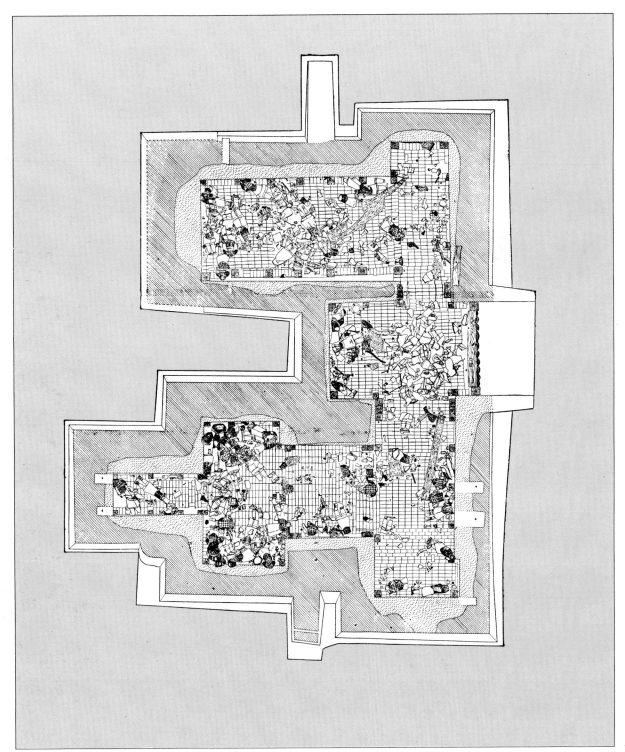

59. *Map on No.3 Pit*

60. *A Terra-cotta Cavalryman and a Terra-cotta Saddled Horse*

59

61

62

56

63

64

65

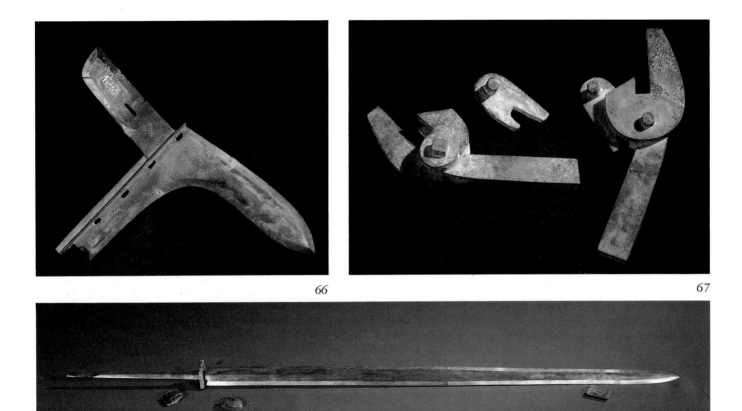

66. *A Bronze Barbed Spear*

67. *Bronze Crossbow Triggers*

68. *A Bronze Sword*

SPLENDID TREASURE-HOUSE OF ANCIENT SCULPTURE

The pits of the terra-cotta armoured warriors and horses form an ancient treasure-house imbued not only with rich military concepts, but also with splendid sculptural art. As a contingent of full-length sculptures of the Qin Dynasty, they are rarely found in the sculptural histories of China and even of the world in so far as rigourism in design, magnitude in scale, vividness in image and exquisite craftsmanship in moulding are concerned.

China's sculptural art has a long history and a fine national tradition. As far back as in the neolithic epoch of the primitive society, there were already painted pottery human heads of small size. From the Dynasties of Shang and Zhou down to the Spring and Autumn Period and the Warring States Period, there were no lack of vivid and graceful sculptures in fascinating expressiveness. However, it was not until the terra-cotta armoured warriors and horses were unearthed that we witnessed the most splendid display in the history of China's sculpture. Nearly 8,000 life-size sculptures of the terra-cotta armoured warriors and horses are arrayed in imitation of the Qin battle formation in the three pits totalling more than 20,000 sq.m. The terra-cotta armoured warriors are 1.8 to 2 m. high while the terra-cotta horses are about 2 m. long. The grandiose lay-out of so large an army in such tremendous momentum presents a striking artistic appeal of conquest and invincibility.

As viewed from the 1,000 odd unearthed terra-cotta armoured warriors and horses, the realistic approach brought the sculptures closer to life prototypes, whether in shape or in manner. The sculpted warriors wear different facial expressions ranging from ponderation, dexterity, simplicity and unaffectedness to naivete, concentration, smiling and anxiety, without a pair in duplication. Portrayed obviously from the true life, the different facial expressions suggest different ages, nationalities, social strata, class origins as well as individualities and innermost thoughts.

Although the terra-cotta armoured warriors and horses survived the catastrophic conflagration and withstood underground moisture and soil erosion of over 2,000 years, colours can still be spotted sticking to some of these figures. A dozen of mineral dyestuffs used include bright red, pink, powder green, powder purple, sky blue, orange yellow, black, white and umber, the most being red, green, blue and umber. The sharp contrast between the warm colours and the cool ones that were painted on them set the keynote of liveliness and magnificence. Just imagine what gorgeous colours such a huge army presents. This, on one hand, reflects the aesthetic views of the Qin people, and on the other hand, deliberately or unintentionally weakens the innate atmosphere of solemnness and horror in works of art on military themes, thus bringing about thrilling scenes of abounding vitality, high morale and all-conquering bravery.

Moreover, a number of crafts were applied in pottery-making, with moulding as the mainstay to be supplemented by heaping-up, hand-shaping, carving and painting. The modelling of the pottery warriors and horses was vivid and precise. They were baked in kilns under an accurate control of contraction tolerance at the temperatures approximately between 950° and 1,050° C. The finished pottery figures looked all the more elegant with pure lustre, high density and great solidity, and gave out clanging sounds when knocked. This shows that China's pottery-making craftsmanship already reached the consummate level 2,200 years ago.

In one word, the terra-cotta armoured warriors and horses appear like a bright pearl in the history of ancient Chinese sculpture. They also take up an important place in the history of the world's fine arts. They can be matched with any time-honoured art treasures in ancient Greece, Rome or elsewhere in the world. As a great thinker says, when commenting on the Greek art, that the artistic value of the terra-cotta armoured warriors and horses today "still gives us great enjoyment, and in certain aspects sets up a norm or a prototype that can not be overtopped."

70. *Side View of Vanguard of Battle Formation in No.1 Pit*

70

73

73. *Terra-cotta Warriors in Battle Tunics*

74. *A Terra-cotta Officer and Array of Terra-cotta Warriors*

75. *A Terra-cotta General*

76. *A Terra-cotta Officer in Armour*

75

68

77

78

80. A Terra-cotta General in
    Battle Tunic

81. A Terra-cotta Warrior

80

81

72

82. *A Terra-cotta Officer*

83. 84. *Belt Hook of a Terra-cotta Warrior in Battle Tunic*

83

82

84

85–88. *Mottled Head of a*
Terra-cotta Warrior

89-92. *Mottled Head of a*
Terra-cotta Warrior

93

94

95

96

93–96. *Head of a Terra-cotta*
    Warrior

97. 98. *Head of a Terra-cotta*
    General

99. 100. *Face of a Terra-cotta General*

101. *Eyes and Eyebrows of a Terra-cotta General*

102. *Mouth, Moustache and Beard of a Terra-cotta General*

99

100

101

102

103

104

*106–111. Head of a Terra-
cotta Warrior*

*112. Hair Style of a Terra-cotta
General*

*113–114. Hair Style of a Terra-
cotta Warrior*

*115. Hair Style of a Terra-
cotta Figure*

106

107

108

109

110

111

112

113

114

115

85

116. 117. *Hand Moulding of a Terra-cotta Figure*

118. 119. *Material-like Armour*

120. 121. *Hand of a Terra-cotta Figure*

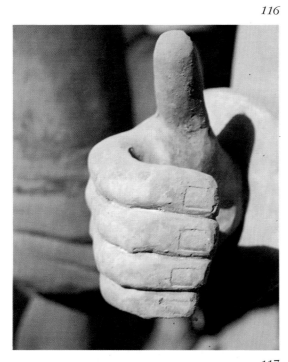

122

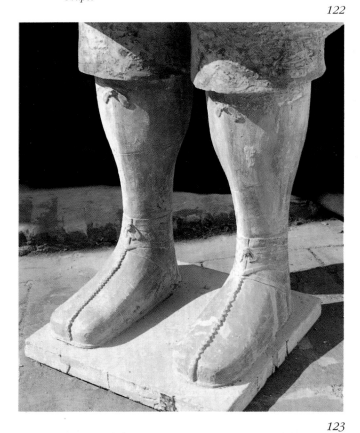

124

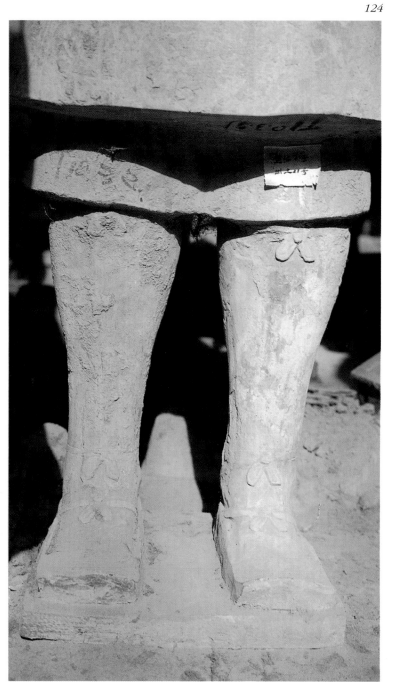

123

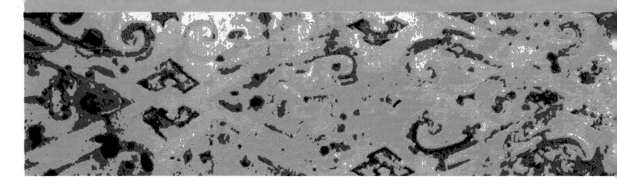

BRONZE CHARIOTS AND HORSES — ACME OF BRONZES

In December 1980, the bronze chariots and horses were excavated in an attendant burial pit 20 m. west to the mound of Qin Shi Huang Mausoleum. The two sets, almost half the actual size, were found facing west, one preceeding the other, in a big wooden coffin about 7 m. long and 2.3 m. wide. Although they are distinctly burial objects of no practical value, the composition of the chariots, the attire of the charioteers and the ornaments on the horses are imitations in every way after the real ones. They are genuine miniatures and reproductions of the chariots and horses used exclusively by the royal family.

Drawn by four bronze horses, each of the two bronze chariots, with a single shaft and two wheels, shows differences in shape and function. The front chariot (No.1 Bronze Chariot and Horses), named the chariot with higher canopy or the chariot without seats, was to lead the fleet of imperial chariots and horses when Qin Shi Huang went on a tour of inspection. The carriage is in a rectangular shape, 1.26 m. wide and 0.70 m. long, topped with a round bronze umbrella of 1.22 m. in diameter, under which stands a bronze charioteer, a long sword at the waist. On the carriage are also a pair of bronze shields, a crossbow and a quiver containing 66 bronze arrows. The four horses, lining abreast, are painted white all over. Each of them is approximately 0.90 m. high and 1.10 m. long. The horses are haltered in silver and gold headstalls, with silver curb bit in the mouth, gold ornaments in the center of the forehead and tassels tied under the neck. The two outside horses have silver and gold straps fastened around their necks. The other two horses in the middle are yoked to bear the shaft. The four horses, fleshy and muscular, have their manes cut short and tails tied. They stand with heads raised as if ready to gallop at a whip from the charioteer.

The back chariot (No.2 Bronze Chariot and Horses), called the chariot with seats or the chariot with beds, has a total length of 3.17 m. and a height of 1.06 m., weighing 1,241 kg. The convex-shaped carriage comprises two compartments. The front compartment is for the charioteer, and the rear one, for the emperor. The carriage is enclosed with wooden boards on the four sides. In the front is a horizontal bar to lean against, and in the back, a door. There is a window on either side of the carriage as well as in the front. The whole carriage is covered by an arched elliptical umbrella. The bronze charioteer in the front compartment, wearing a long robe and a doubled-tailed hat, sits on his knees to a height of 0.51 m., a short sword at the waist and his hands stretched out holding reins. With a smiling face and concentration of mind, the charioteer looks care-free, content and cautious to be a fine bronze sculpture of rare value.

The bronze chariots and horses possess very high artistic value. The carriages and canopies of the two imperial chariots are painted all over with various bright-coloured patterns resembling cloud, *Kui* (legendary one-legged dragon-like animal) and phoenix. On many other parts and accessories are painted with geometric patterns of rhombuses, squares and triangles in inlaying silver and gold threads. They symbolize rolling clouds, curling mists, flying dragons or dancing phoenixes. Inlaid with fine and smooth lines, they look sumptuous yet simple and elegant, and at the same time appear gorgeous yet solemn and serious. This reflects from one angle the topmost respect and honour of the emperor — the master of the chariots. The vivid precise modelling and lefe-like images of the bronze horses and the bronze charioteers are acclaimed as the acme of artistic perfection.

The technological process in making the bronze chariots and horses also attained an incredibly high level. The No.2 Bronze Chariot and Horses alone has 3,462 components of various sizes, of which 1,700 odd are silver and gold pieces. The whole process involves casting, welding, sticking, chiseling, carving, polishing and inlaying, out of which quite a few are inventions by craftsmen of the Qin Dynasty. To give a couple of examples, the spokes are installed in the hub of the wheel by means of interference fit, i.e. the spokes are forced into the slots of the preheated hub, and many of the ornamental pieces are decorated with chains made of bronze wires that have an even thickness of 0.5 millimeters all the length. Observed under a magnifier, the chains do not bear forging traces. Obviously, the wire-drawing technique was applied. This holds an extremely important value in the history of technology. Many of the components on the carriages are assembled in a rational and scientific way. Take for example the component used to fix the umbrella pole erect on the No.1 Bronze Chariot and Horses. A slight pull at the key opens the locker. When closed, the locker is automatically restored to its former position under the weight of the key, thus locking the umbrella pole fast in the key-hole. The fit is so tight and flawless that it is really a wonder.

As was recorded in China's historical books, Qin Shi Huang made five nation-wide tours during his reign. Accompanied by a large retinue, the grand procession "comprised 81 sets of magnificent chariots and horses, with the emperor's own carriage surrounded in the center...." The discovery of the bronze chariots and horses makes the grand occasion of the imperial procession of Qin Shi Huang seen through the real objects and provides precious substantial materials to know and study the ancient imperial chariot institution. It also fully reflects China's superb technological level in metalworking over 2,000 years ago and the fine wisdom and great talents of the ancient Chinese labouring people. The bronze chariots and horses may be well rated as "the crown of the bronzes".

125. Excavation of Bronze
Chariots and Horses

126

126. *Excavation of No.1*
    Bronze Chariot and
    Horses

127. *Excavation of No.2*
    Bronze Chariot and
    Horses

127

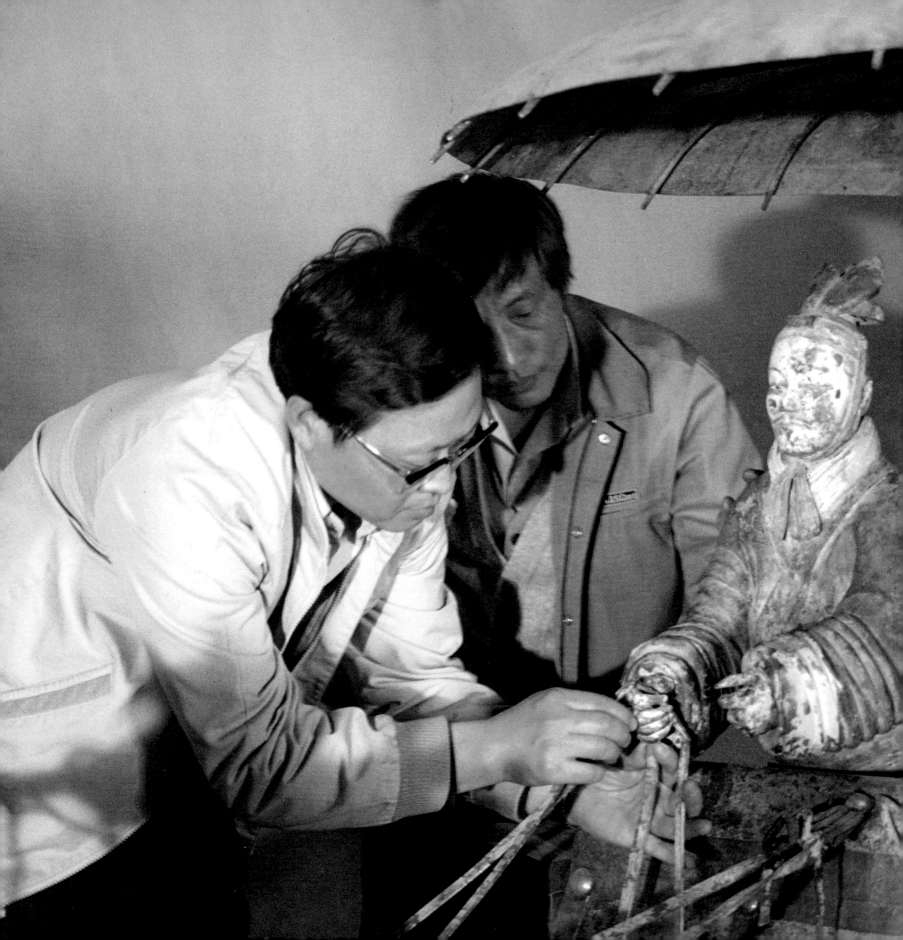

128

*128. No.1 Bronze Chariot and
Horses under Repair*

*129. Bronze Charioteer of No.2
Bronze Chariot*

129

130

131

133

134

135

137

139. Bronze Outside Horse on
    Right

140. Close-up of Bronze
    Outside Horse on Right

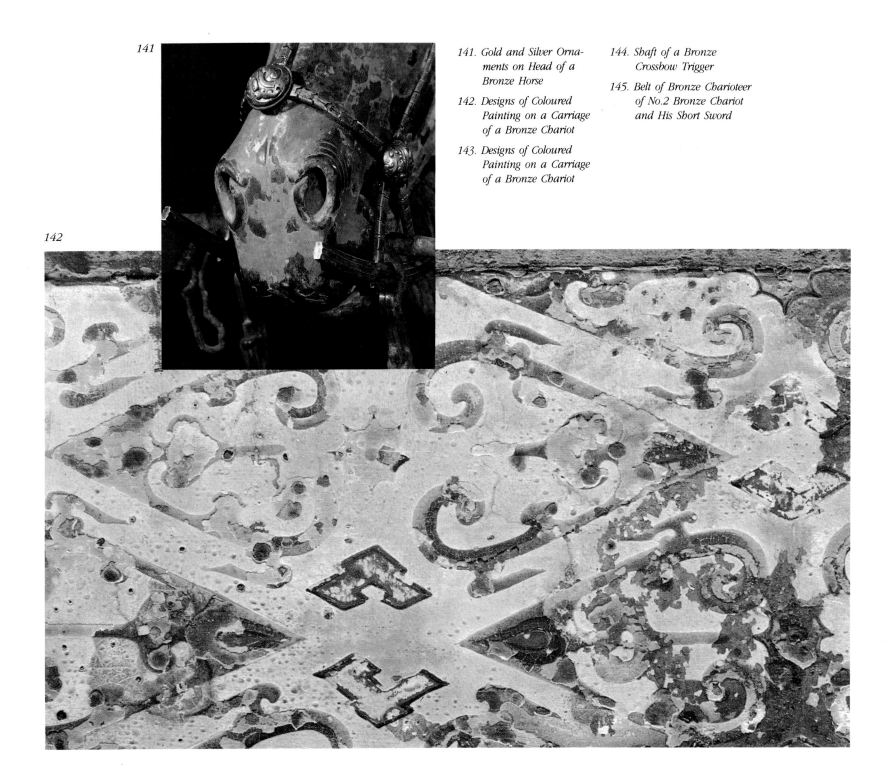

141. Gold and Silver Ornaments on Head of a Bronze Horse

142. Designs of Coloured Painting on a Carriage of a Bronze Chariot

143. Designs of Coloured Painting on a Carriage of a Bronze Chariot

144. Shaft of a Bronze Crossbow Trigger

145. Belt of Bronze Charioteer of No.2 Bronze Chariot and His Short Sword

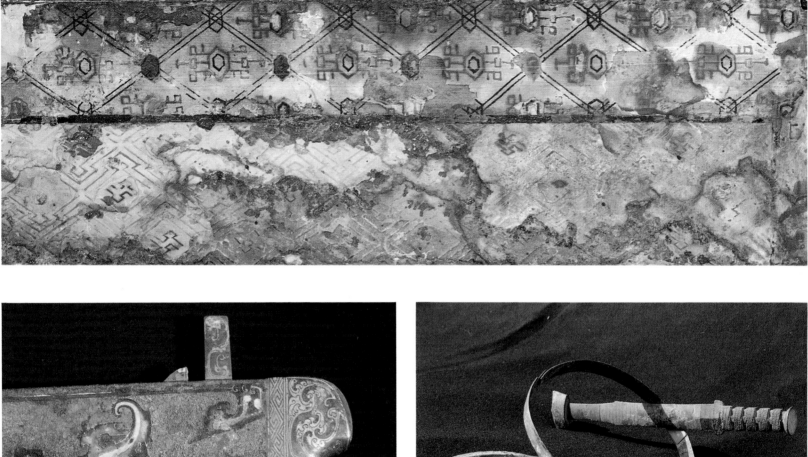

144

145

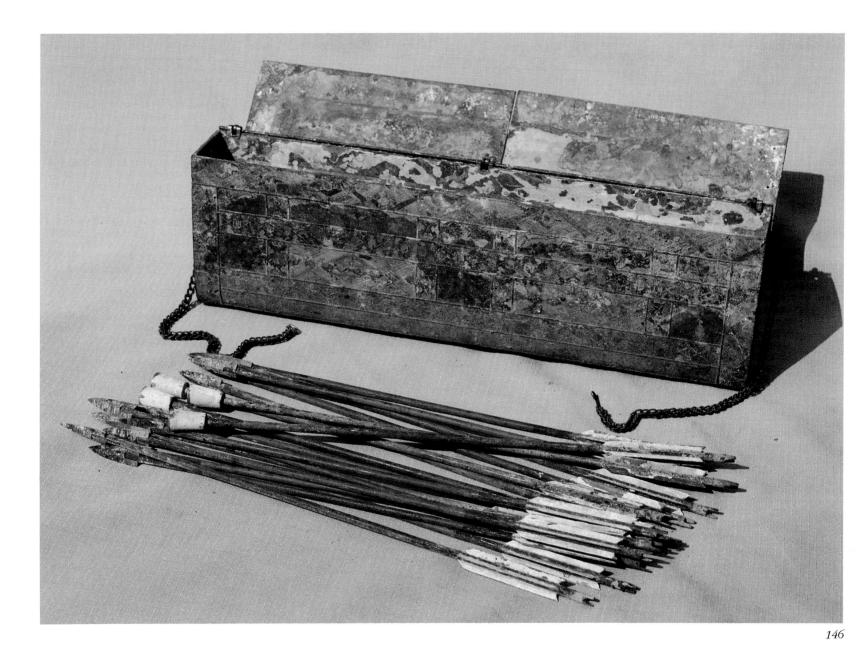

146

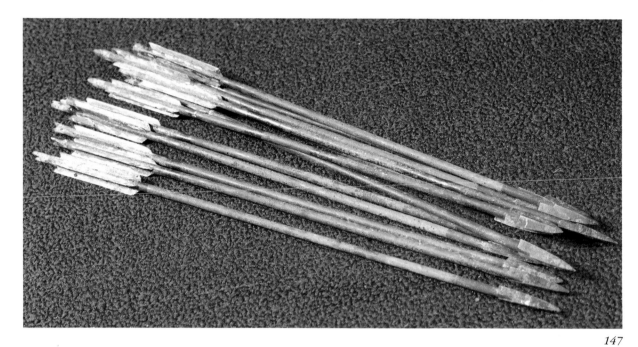

147

146. *A Quiver and Arrows*

147. *Arrow-heads*

148. *Close-up of Arrows' Tails*

148

149

110

151. A Chariot Wheel

151

112

VALIANT IMPERIAL WARRIORS 2,200 YEARS AGO

—Terra-cotta Armoured Warriors and Horses of
Qin Shi Huang Mausoleum

Chief Editor: Wu Xiaocong

Editor: Shi Guolin

Written by: Wu Xiaocong

Translated by: Lu Zuben

Checked by: Zhou Longru   Lu Zuben

Photoed by: Guo Youmin   Gao Yuying   Xia Juxian   Guo Yan

Designed by: Shi Guolin

Published by: Xi'an World Publishing Corporation

Distributed by: CHINA NATIONAL PUBLICATIONS IMPORT & EXPORT
CORPORATION, XI'AN BRANCH
17 Nan Da Jie,
Xi'an 710001, China

Publishing date: March, 2000.

ISBN: 7 – 5062 – 2622 – 7/G • 39